Self-Publishing

with

Stellium

How to Produce a Better Book

Sasha Fenton

First published in 2017 in the UK by Stellium Ltd
Plymouth, Devon (UK)
Tel: +44 (0)1752 367 300   Fax: +44 (0)1752 350 453
email: stelliumpub@gmail.com   www.stelliumpub.com

British Library Cataloguing in Publication Data:
A catalogue record for this book is available from the British Library

ISBN: 978-0-9575783-9-5
Illustrations copyright © 2017 Jan Budkowski,
Adobe Stock Photos and others
Typesetting by Zambezi Publishing Ltd
Printed in the UK by Lightning Source UK

Contents

We can Help You Achieve your Dream!

It has never been easier to get a book "out there", but for many people, the technicalities involved in producing a book appear overwhelming, while the business side of publishing is a complete mystery. We at Stellium can help you to overcome these problems and bring your words, ideas and dreams into the light of day.

Developments over the past ten years or more clearly showed an increasing tendency for the book trade to minimise opportunities for authors to get their message out into the public arena, despite an increasingly available and technologically attainable means of literary creation and distribution, world-wide. The rapid change from analogue to digital publishing methods, which also enabled the rise of Print On Demand (POD) availability, enabled authors with just a minimum of computer savvy to self-publish their work at very reasonable cost. The rise of the Amazon Kindle ebook reader added a further step to new freedom of expression, because ebooks mean even more savings in the process of book publishing.

About Stellium

Sasha Fenton and Jan Budkowski realised the need to adapt to changing times, and notwithstanding a long and successfully ongoing publishing career with their Mind, Body and Spirit (MB&S) publishing house – Zambezi Publishing Ltd – it was clearly time to break new ground. The major step was to create a completely new business model, called Stellium Ltd. Stellium is dedicated to all things non-MB&S, including fiction and non-fiction, but mainly attuned to the new model of providing self-publishing services to all those people who either had a manuscript in their bottom drawer, or who hadn't even started to write a book, solely because they believed they had no chance of getting a publishing deal.

There are many authors who have published their own Kindle ebook, or even a printed version of their book. It's perfectly accessible nowadays, both technically and financially!

So, why should we intervene?

The answer is clear to those people who have already produced and put their pet project on sale, usually on Amazon. Or, who have gone from bookshop to bookshop, trying to sell their lovely new book - a project on which they have spent months or years writing and rewriting. These people know that the result has been:

- Loads of critical reviews on Amazon about their poor spelling, grammar, style, lack of creativity, amateurish covers and prices totally out of kilter with the content on offer.
- Rejection by bookshops, total silence from W. H. Smith and Waterstones
- Minimal direct sales to friends and colleagues, notwithstanding glowing encouragement during the writing process.

The next step for those authors is a rush to find out: why the disaster? Amazon reviews, if any, help in pointing out the errors, but they don't give a complete list. Bookshop owners could add more guidance, but they don't need to – they can choose from over two hundred thousand new titles published every year in the UK alone by conventional publishers. Bookshop owners know an amateurish job even before they open the book; they are experts in their business.

So, what is the overall problem for the self-published author? Well, it's the same as someone deciding to perform brain surgery on the basis that scalpels are now affordable, ignoring the fact that the real surgeon has spent years in training and practising his skills. Add to that simple answer the additional fact that there are so many books out there nowadays, with a million or more new self-published titles every year in addition to the conventionally published ones and you get the idea. Here is a simple but inescapable fact of life:

- Taking over the means of producing a book doesn't get rid of all the tasks involved in the publishing process – those tasks simply pass onto the author's shoulders.

What follows in this book helps to explain not just the pricing of our services, but also the tasks that are necessary to distinguish an amateurish job from a polished work that the author can rightly be proud of.

We provide the know-how, the technology and resources to turn out a professional level book. All this requires a high level of experience and a lot of expensive software for page layout, design elements, image creation and enhancement, other publishing resources, contacts for sales and distribution, and maintaining a constant eye on developments and critical insider knowledge.

All the above still needs more; promotion and marketing are in constant need, and we can help our authors in this respect as well.

We differ from many other self-publishing service providers in two important ways:

- First of all, we have learnt that the average writer doesn't really wish to know all the things that go on behind the scenes. He or she just wants his manuscript patted nicely into shape. Quite right too - either you write or you publish; each is a skill in its own right. Similarly, you don't want to know how your calculator works and what's inside it – you just want it to calculate, so that you can get on with more important things.
- Secondly, Sasha is a well-established author in her own right, having written over 130 books for traditional publishers and for

herself, with total international sales in excess of 6.5 million copies. She has an in-depth knowledge of both sides of the equation, as a writer and a publisher.

Who better to deal with your project?

This book has become an essential tool, because we found ourselves spending so much time explaining the whys and wherefores to our authors that it was taking up time that could be better spent on useful work. It was initially intended as a short, simple leaflet, but it turns out that there is so much involved – like the tip of an iceberg – that it's now a decent sized book, free to our signed up authors, but also available as an ebook and printed version for a small price on Amazon.

If you find this book helpful, please tell your friends so that they can improve their own chances when they decide to write a book a book!

Self-Publishing with Stellium

Overview

You have written a book and now you want to turn it into a printed book or an ebook or both. Maybe your manuscript is a personal memoir or a book of poetry, a novel or a children's book, or perhaps a photographic record of some event in your life, or even a training manual for your workshops. The self-publishing system works well for all of these topics and many more as well.

Getting conventional publishers to accept a debut novel is extremely difficult, and famous examples of successful authors who had trouble with their first books are J. K. Rowling with her Harry Potter series, which was rejected 18 times before Bloomsbury took it on, and Stephen King's first novel, *Carrie,* was rejected by 30 publishers before one finally took a chance on it. Self-publishing can be useful here, as happened with E. L. James and her *Fifty Shades of Grey,* and Sasha Fenton herself, who has self-published many books over the years, often seeing them picked up later and energetically marketed by large publishers.

What would my book cost me?

A simple question, but it begs a very long answer, and that's why we decided to produce this book. Our lives would be much simpler if we just gave you a few package deals to choose from, as do many other publishers. We tried that at first, but we soon found that some books involve much more work than others, so we would have to make the package prices higher to start with. Also, many books had to be changed, shortened or somehow forced into a container that didn't really work. Secondly, there are so many details that first-time writers aren't aware of, and that they later discover they actually need, that we were ending up with unhappy authors.

So, we changed to a "menu" system and we freely give you our advice about your project, to help you achieve your objective, with no hidden costs or traps involved. Furthermore, we don't involve you in any costs without your prior approval.

This means that, we can only give you an accurate quote once you have chosen the services that you want from the "menu", and we have assessed your project, using our "Think Form" and a few pages of your manuscript (kindly don't send us the full manuscript until we call for it.)

What we can do right now is to give you a sample cost for an average novel that doesn't need much (if any) repair work, and just doing the normal work that is involved in the publishing process.

This novel might have about 60,000 words, black and white content with no photos or images, full colour front and back covers plus the spine, and allowing for a cover image or photo from the author if desired. This kind of project would cost about £400. Printing costs would be about £2.40 per copy, with the addition of the printer's one-off setup fees of £50 (incl. VAT), a local market / archive fee of £8.40 (incl. VAT) and our 15% admin fees. An optional but important extra is a one-off advert in the biggest wholesaler's catalogue in the western world - Ingrams. This costs £60 plus VAT and a 15% admin fee, and is distributed worldwide to over 27,000 bookshops and other retailers.

I repeat, this is a very general pricing example, but it gives you a fair idea of the price range for an average book. We charge more for non-fiction titles, as there is more work involved, and there are more charges if you want your book to be professionally edited. Nevertheless, the self publishing process nowadays is well and truly accessible as never before.

You will find all the information you need to know, and how to cost your project, in the following pages. We welcome any other questions you may have, so don't hesitate to email or phone us - our details are at the back of this book.

Do we take any kind of book?
Please note that Stellium reserves the right to refuse to accept certain types of material. For example, we don't accept porn, libel, or racist books.

The Stellium "Think Form"
Books come in all shapes and sizes, and the work involved in producing them can vary enormously, so the first thing we do is issue our Think Form, which allows you to consider your requirements, while also showing us what you have in mind. The Think Form isn't a contract and it doesn't commit you to anything. If you aren't sure about anything that you see on the Think Form, please leave that section blank, and if you aren't sure what would be best for your book, please ask us for any information that you require.

Do I need every part of the process?
No. There are several steps that need to be taken to complete the publishing process, but you may not need all of them. Please read through this guide, check out the processes and the options and look at the separate Price Guide to get some idea of what each stage costs.

Ebooks
We can produce an ebook for you, either instead of a printed book or in addition to one, and you don't have to produce both types of book at the same time. Factors related to book production make it best to prepare and make up the printed version and add on the ebook shortly after or at some later time.

There are two advantages to an ebook, the first being that it is instantly available all over the world and doesn't need to be posted to the customer, while the second is that there is no printing involved, which makes it a cheap option. The disadvantages are that you can't charge much for an ebook, and secondly, there is no lovely paper copy for you to give to your family and friends.

Tarot, oracle and other cards

We can produce small quantities of cards in specially made boxes – say 100 decks at a time. You will see more about this in a later chapter.

Please remember that if you are VAT registered, some products may require VAT on top of the retail price. CDs and other additions may come into this category. Ebooks are also involved, but Amazon deals with this for all Kindle ebooks.

Remember...

You are the publisher and Stellium Ltd is the facilitator but you will find loads of money-saving tips in our guide. We can make your book available worldwide, but as with any book, however it is published, it is always up to the author to put some effort into marketing.

DETAILS

Honour your work

Writing takes a great deal of effort, yet to our surprise many authors are more interested in getting something for nothing than in honouring their work by having a decent job done. You will find other publishing houses who will merely reduce the size of your typed manuscript, put some kind of cover on it, give it an ISBN and call it a book, but a Microsoft Word manuscript isn't a book, and the shops and online stores won't touch this kind of product, and nobody else will think much of it either.

Self-publishing with Stellium

We at Stellium have made a conscious decision to maintain a high standard of work, but you are the publisher, and it is up to you to choose the options that you want to finance and to leave out those that you don't. In this guide, we offer you lots of suggestions that will help you produce a really great book, while also saving money, and you will find our prices really reasonable.

Editing

Fact one: All conventional publishers use freelance editors and these people need to be properly paid, because their job requires skill and knowledge, and it takes time to do the job properly. Editing is a relatively expensive option, but no conventional publisher would dream of putting a book on the market without having it professionally edited, and even hugely successful authors often owe a great deal to their editors.

Fact two: Only a very small number of self-published authors choose to have their books edited, and the results of this corner-cutting decision are often all too apparent - although we offer useful tips that can help authors to overcome the editing problem without breaking the bank.

Fact three: Please bear in mind that the material that you send us will become your book – whatever the condition of the grammar, typing and style. Also, please use common sense. One author decided to do without the editing option, but later said she had left out all the punctuation in her manuscript because she assumed we would put it in for her!

Covers

As long as it is within the bounds of possibility, you can choose the type of cover you want and even help to design it yourself. You can choose a shiny finish or matte-laminate paperback or you can choose a hardback.

Printing

Most of our books are produced by the print-on-demand (POD) method, which means that you can run off any quantity that you want from one copy upwards, and you can reprint whenever you want. The setup and first print run takes a couple of weeks, while reprints take a few days. We ask our printer to run off one copy for your approval, and if it is all right, to go ahead with printing the quantity that you require. If changes need to be made, we arrange for this to be done and then we ask the printer to run off another copy for you to check over.

A previously published book

You may wish to revive and republish a book that has been previously published. Please see more about this later, in the Copyright chapter.

Copyright

You always retain the copyright to your work unless you specifically agree to part with it. Stellium won't ask you to give up your copyright.

Your profit margin

You keep all the profit from your book once the cost of printing, postage and our small admin fee have been cleared. Bookshops, Internet / online retailers and distributors all take their cut, but this is the case for every publisher, whether conventional or self-pub.

An ISBN

If your book is a paper book, we can organise an ISBN for you (International Standard Book Number). This will make your book available to any person or any shop anywhere in the world. If your book is only meant for your family and friends, you won't need an ISBN. You don't need an ISBN for an ebook.

Withholding tax

The USA Internal Revenue Service (IRS) claims thirty per cent of any USA-based income, unless you register with them and prove that you pay income in the UK. We can help you with such issues.

Legal deposit

It's mandatory to furnish the British Library (and possibly five other deposit libraries) with copies of your book if it has an ISBN. We can deal with this requirement for you.

Publisher's jargon

- A manuscript or typescript is often referred to as an MS.
- Indie-publishing, self-publishing, assisted publishing, self-pub, and partnership publishing all mean the same thing.
- We often refer to print-on-demand as "digital printing" or "POD".

The publisher's mantra is:

"We can publish a book quickly, cheaply or well"
Publishers can sometimes manage two of the above,
most of the time only one, but never all three at once,
so please consider your real needs.

How Much will it Cost to Print my Book?

OVERVIEW

When people approach us, often their first question is "How much would it cost to print my book?" Well there's a lot more to publishing a book than merely printing it, and in the case of an ebook, there isn't any printing at all, but many things have to happen before a book and its cover are in a format that can be sent to a printer or made into an ebook. Please see the separate price sheet listing the average costs for the various elements of book production at this time. It's worth bearing in mind that you may not want or need every part of the process, and the more you can do for yourself the cheaper the job becomes.

As far as money is concerned, here are two points that you might wish to consider:

1)   If you can take a week's holiday and consider taking a second holiday in the same year without feeling any financial strain, you can easily afford to publish your book.

2)   Stellium asks for payment in two parts for the preparation process, while the print charges are added later, as a separate issue, so you don't have to find all the money at once.

DETAILS

Please see the enclosed Price Guide to get an idea of the cost of the various processes involved in publishing a book. If the guide is missing, then call us and ask for a copy.

How Much will it Cost to Print my Book?

Money saving tips

If you absolutely cannot afford to publish your book but you still want something on paper, you can design a cover and put it onto a memory stick along with the contents of your book, take the memory stick to your local quick-print shop and ask them to print as many copies as you need and to ring-bind them for you. Nevertheless, always check the costs involved before signing anything.

Perhaps you have noticed the £99 ebook deals that you see advertised in writing magazines or on the Net? When you read the requirements, you will see that the publisher needs a fully finalised, edited, typeset and formatted MS Word file that is the right shape and layout for an ebook, including a front cover, blurb and so on. If you are skilled enough for this and if it suits you, and as long as your book doesn't contain illustrations, graphics, tables or any other complications, we can match the £99 price. However, as with an iceberg, there is more involved beneath the surface in preparing a book for publication, whether as an ebook or a paper book, than may appear to be the case. Check with us, as our £99 offers may not always be available.

Tarot and other cards

We can help you to produce a deck of colour-illustrated cards and a matching box to keep them in. These can be viably printed in relatively small quantities, from 100 decks upwards. Depending upon the amount of work involved and the number of cards in the deck, the initial cost would range from £1,000 for 100 sets. Reprints should cost less.

However, one should be really, really sure about being able to sell the cards directly, otherwise the investment could be a waste of money. If you do produce a deck and it sells very well (congratulations!), then it's good to know that bigger print runs can significantly reduce the per-set cost. Importantly, if your deck design does become very popular, it would be sensible to consider licensing the design to an established card manufacturer, because there are risks in taking on a major investment if you don't have all the peripheral necessities in hand. Necessities such as local and overseas distributors and sales teams, contacts with major bookshops and other outlets, and extensive management and marketing skills.

Having said all this, you might still want to produce a deck of cards for your group, friends, clients or for yourself - if so, then discuss your project with us.

Copyright

Your copyright

Everything you write is your copyright, unless you choose to sell it to someone else. It's a good idea to publish your work promptly, making it easier to establish the year of its creation. The 1911 Act provides that an individual's work is automatically under copyright, by operation of law, as soon as it leaves his/her mind and is embodied in some physical form. Proof is the essence, so publishing is a good method of "embodying in physical form" your work. The well-known idea of sealing a copy in an envelope and mailing it to yourself is less than adequate, because it isn't foolproof; for example, an unsealed envelope can be mailed, and then sealed at a later date.

Other people's copyright

Copyright is a really tricky subject and even skilled writers aren't always sure about it, so the best course of action is to ensure that everything inside your book and on the cover is original. Copyright exists in the expression of an idea – not the idea itself. An expressed set of words, illustrations, photographs, sketches and music are all protected by copyright, as is everything you find on the Internet. In general, copyright ends seventy years after the death of the author, illustrator or composer. Ask us about copyright matters if you have any doubts. Our initial answer will be to keep things as simple as possible, because copyright legislation is very complex. A good resource to show you the range of issues is the "Copyright law of the United Kingdom" page in Wikipedia. Keep in mind that there may be changes in applicable law, and that

Wikipedia is not the law itself, nor is it necessarily always up to date, so it's best to obtain written permissions from the author / owner / publisher, or else to steer clear of other people's work.

DETAILS

Quotations

People love to use quotations from other authors, but you need written permission from the original writer and / or publisher to use their words in your book. An acknowledgement isn't enough. Some publishers charge a fee for this. The doctrine of fair dealing exists, but this is also a complex matter.

Music

The music world is very quick to jump on anything, so even a few words quoted from a song can be dangerous, as music publishers will sue everyone concerned, including the author, publisher and even the bookshop. Please get written permission from the composers and music publishers or leave the quotation out. Hymns and old folk songs are often fine –but ensure that the copyright has long since run out! Always check the position carefully.

Illustrations

Even using a tiny piece of someone's illustration will land you in difficulties. Illustrations, diagrams and other such work always need written permission from the artist, and if appropriate, also from the publisher. The legend has it that if you change 10% of the artwork, that is enough to avoid copyright issues. The fact is, even changing 50% gives you no rights. A better idea is to use the test of having someone look at your version and objectively decide whether it could have been developed from the original.

Photographs

Permission will be needed from the photographer before you can use any photo, and this even applies to studio photos of you. Photos taken by you on your own camera or by a family member are fine.

The Internet
Anything on the Internet is copyright even when it says it isn't. In theory, you could take something that says it's non-copyright for a club newsletter but that's all.

Book titles
Oddly enough, book titles aren't copyright, but you won't want to promote someone else's book rather than your own, so use your own imagination rather then copying someone else's work. Check

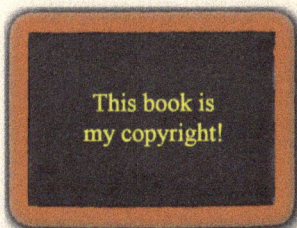

on amazon.co.uk, amazon.com and do a Google search to see if your title is already in use.

Changes in the law
We in publishing are very familiar with the concept of copyright where it relates to text. The rule is that copyright extends for 70 years after the death of the author, and only after that does the work fall into the "public domain", which means that parts of the book can be used without the permission of the author, his executor or his previous publisher. Until recently, the rule for artwork was that copyright only extended for 25 years after the

work was first created, but now the rule for artwork is the same as it is for text.

The word "design" relates to anything that can be designed, so it might be furniture, an engineering concept, patterned wallpaper and of course, artistic work. For instance, if you want to show a particular piece of furniture or a garden design in your book to illustrate a point, you will now need the permission of the creator or his executor if he is no longer alive. This makes it even more imperative that you avoid taking anything from the Internet, because you can't always check its provenance. Whereas, on the other hand, software is available that will swiftly find copied material online, and inform those who might be inclined to sue.

The Intellectual Property Office did give authors, web designers and business owners a six month transition period, but this ended on the 28th of January 2017. Now, copyright owners can take legal action for copyright infringement.

Go to http:/bit.ly/2c27PAd for more information.

This may cause a problem for those authors, publishers and self-publishers who already have books on the market that contain photographs of things that someone has designed. Some things that immediately come to mind are those cheapy books on Feng Shui that included photographic images of houses, furniture and gardens.

A previously published book

Sometimes people ask us to re-publish a book that was previously published either by a conventional publisher or with the help of another self-publishing firm. This is perfectly acceptable, but there are a few things that need to be done first, and these apply just as much to a self-published book as they do to a conventionally published book.

Firstly, the text and any images will have been licensed to the previous publisher or self-publishing company, and these rights will need to revert to the author. This is a simple matter for the author to write to the publisher and request a reversion of rights, and then wait for their letter to come back, saying this has been done. Secondly, the typesetting, formatting and design of the book are copyright to whoever worked on it, and depending upon circumstances, this might be the publisher or even the freelance technician who did the actual work. In plain English, this means that the layout of the pages is copyright, so it can't simply be scanned and put out onto the market again in its original format.

If the author has the original text and images stored on his or her own computer or on disc, then once the rights have been cleared, we can start the whole process from that point. The only benefit comes if the text had been edited to the author's satisfaction, which means that it won't need to be done again. If the book is not on disc, we can get it scanned. Scanning puts a host of artefacts into and around the text, so the author or a copy editor will have to carefully copy-edit the text onto a disc, and the layout will need to be changed so that it isn't the same as the original. The copyright page and a few other things will need to be replaced. This might actually be a good thing in its way, because the author might want to take the opportunity to update the book and add new information. The cover will be replaced, because the cover design copyright will definitely belong to the previous designer.

Old books that are out of print will still be hanging around in cyber space, so there may be old versions of your book offered by traders who are selling off their stocks, while there may also be second hand copies floating around. There is not much you can do about this, but it shouldn't affect the sales of the new book. The word "sales" is itself a tricky matter though, because some authors think that a change of publisher or self-publisher will automatically result in a massive increase in sales. The fact is that the book will need a renewed marketing boost.

Taking things further, old books tend to have poor covers, because the designs would have been done by hand in the pre-computer age, and they may have been done cheaply, produced in a rush and poorly executed or in dull colours. In this case, a fresh cover might help to create some renewed interest. Sometimes the typesetting inside old books is very poor (or even non-existent in the case of those publishers who merely slap an indifferent cover onto the author's word file), so a professionally produced look will make the book much more palatable to booksellers. Either way, republishing a book is a gamble, but it may be worth it.

One area where it is definitely worth updating a book or bringing back an old book is when a subject suddenly becomes more important than it was when the first book came out. An example of this is Sasha's current book on Diabetes. She is now updating this, because in the decade since writing the original, she has learned more about managing the ailment, and diabetes itself has become far more prevalent. There are now more than three million registered diabetics in the UK, and the figure, like obesity, grows every year.

What we Need You to Send to Us

DETAILS

The Think Form

The first thing we will ask for is our Think Form, which enables us to see what you want. We can send you a paper copy, or we can email it as a PDF attachment.

A copy of our Think Form is included at the end of this book. The Think Form is frequently updated, but even if this version is a little out of date, it gives you a very good idea of what we need to know in order to put together a quote for your project!

An outline and sample pages

We require a synopsis and a few sample pages so we can better understand your book, and so we can work out a quotation for you. Don't send us the complete manuscript unless we ask for it.

Sending in the manuscript

We will send you a quotation and if you are happy to proceed, we will ask for the whole book. The file can be in MS Word, OpenOffice or even PageFour format, and it's easiest to send it to us as an email attachment. Alternatively, use a flash drive, CD or floppy disc. Ensure that your text has been edited as best you can, and that nothing is missing or in the wrong place. Just remember that presenting your book in the best light is important, especially if you hope to get it into bookshops.

Graphics

You can send us a printout or even hand sketches to show us where you want graphics, illustrations or photos to go, if relevant. Probably the best route is to insert a line starting with "zzz" and a comment saying which image should go there. Name each image by sticking a post-it note on the back so that you don't damage it.

- Don't embed images or other artwork in the Word file, the resolution is typically useless for anything but screen or web viewing.
- Send graphical work in a separate folder, marked with post-its on the back and in the correct sequence.
- Check with us about the resolution of graphic material or whether we need the originals.
- Keep copies of everything yourself, and insure important material before sending. If you are worried about using the Royal Mail, use a courier service instead.
- You can photocopy pages from your favourite book to show us the kind of layout and fonts that you like. We may not be able to replicate things exactly, but this will give us a good idea of what you have in mind.
- You can send us a sketch to show how you would like the cover to look, or you can photocopy some other book's cover to give us some inspiration.

Money Saving Tips

OVERVIEW

The more you can do for yourself, the less you will need to pay for, so pull in favours from friends for help with editing and ask friends to help you arrange marketing events.

Remember that you are the publisher, which means that every page of text that you publish will cost you money at every stage, so keep needless waffle down to a minimum. Non-fiction writers often say what they want to say, then say it again and then for good measure repeat it all over again. Avoid this, as it makes the book boring and expensive. In a novel, cut out the slow, philosophical passages and lose the kind of unnecessary detail that slows up the plot. If you want to include acknowledgements in your book, be brief. Look at other books in Waterstones or your local bookshop, and you'll see that the professionals keep things to a minimum.

DETAILS

Typed pages or handwriting

Get handwritten or typed pages entered into a computer and then email the file to us. If this is beyond you, learn how to do this or ask a friend to help you. We can arrange for this to be done, but it would be much cheaper if you can get it done informally. Scanning the pages using OCR (optical character recognition software) is also an option, but not on handwriting, and it is never 100% accurate.

Always back up your digitised work on CD or on a flash drive.

Tablet, laptop, desktop?

It is much easier to write a book on a desktop computer with a proper keyboard and mouse. Tablets aren't much use for writing a whole book, while laptops are an alternative, but why struggle? A desktop is cheaper than an equivalent laptop. We have seen files sent to us where whole lines have become mangled and lost through "laptop syndrome". Much of the book is likely to be disjointed, and an editor will have to guess what you are trying to say while, in effect, rewriting the book. Needless to say, this would be a costly option.

Software

The standard word processing program is Microsoft Word, but cheaper or even free alternatives such as OpenOffice and LibreOffice are becoming popular. Interestingly, Sasha writes all her books (including this one) in a program called PageFour, which is a simplified word processor dedicated to the book writing process. It is cheap to buy, it's amazingly user-friendly and it is very easy for a writer to use. PageFour produces RTF files, which are easily and accurately converted into Microsoft Word's DOC or DOCX format.

Printing

Read the chapter on Printing to see approximately what your book will cost to print. Bear in mind that the overall size of the book and the type of cover will affect the cost, as will the number of pages, so trim any waffle, long-winded descriptions and repetition.

Editing

If you want to do your own editing, print your manuscript (MS) out in at least one-and-a-half spacing and go through it on paper. It's notoriously difficult to see errors on a screen, but they leap into view once the work is printed out. Correct the manuscript, print it out again and give it to a friend. Ask him to read through the text and mark anything that doesn't make sense or that needs rewriting, while also picking up spelling, grammar and typing errors. Make your corrections again and give it to another friend to do the same again. Once you have corrected everything, use the spell and grammar check on your computer again and give your book one last thorough going over.

Proof reading

Once we have typeset your book, we will send you a set of "page proofs". Go these carefully and mark any necessary changes clearly in red ink. There should only be a few small changes, but if you decide to rewrite part or all of the book at this stage, there will be a charge for the time and effort it takes to get the work corrected and to do the design and formatting work again.

Full stops

If you are a typist, you may be accustomed to putting two spaces after a full stop. This has to be changed to one space before starting the page layout process, so when you have finished your book, use your word processor's "Find and Replace" feature to correct the spacing.

Hyphens
Use hyphens to link certain word pairs, such as twenty-one. Many word pairs don't need a hyphen, but those that do will be quite obvious. You can check out various structural and grammatical rules online, with a simple Google search.

Inverted commas
- Use inverted commas (also known as quotation marks) (" ") if you are quoting from another source - take care not to fall foul of copyright.
- You can use single or double inverted commas, but don't use both styles in the same MS.
- Use single inverted commas for contractions, such as don't, won't, it's or to show possession, such as Liam's jacket.
- The possessive case can be tricky, especially where plurals are concerned. If you have a problem with this, the first step is to look up the item online. You can also ask us - we won't send you a bill for helping out with a few words here and there. If you are seriously keen, try a book called: *Eats, Shoots And Leaves*. Once you've read it, you'll understand why it's worth it...

Layout - headers
Many authors love to put headers on every page of their work, giving a host of unnecessary information, including the author's name, the title of the book and an obscure numbering cipher, along with the fact that the work is copyright. These are unnecessary and they have to be removed, which can be difficult in some cases due to software constraints. This adds to your costs, so read our tips carefully.

Procedure Header and Footer

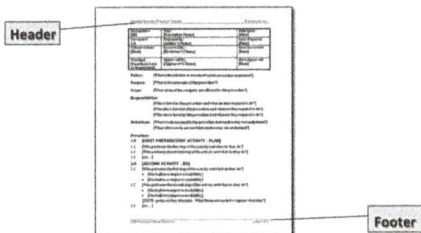

Page numbers

If you know how to do it, insert page numbers in the footers of your MS. It isn't a problem if you don't, but it also helps you to keep track of the pages when you print out the manuscript.

Indents

Tabbed indents, or worse still, indents created by pushing the space bar along several spaces, will have to come out, and some of these features are difficult and time-consuming to remove. Please remove indents and so forth yourself before submitting the MS. By all means, leave a single blank line between paragraphs.

Justified margins

This means margins that are vertically aligned on both left and right sides. They look nice on the screen but they are hard to remove in MS Word, and they keep on jumping back in recent versions of MS Word. Leave your text left-aligned. If you have already justified the margins, undo them and then save your file in RTF format. Then close the file, re-open it and save it as a Word file, preferably as a simpler DOC file instead of the DOCX format, as the latter introduces more unwanted (and hidden) settings than ever!

Centred text

If you want to put a few stars in the middle of a page to separate parts of the book, that's fine, but use the centre option in your word processor instead of tabs or the space bar.

Paragraphs
Show that a paragraph is at an end by hitting enter and leaving a blank line. Do not hit "Alt" and a carriage return or any other strange tweaks on the keyboard, or you will end up with weird, hidden metadata and formatting, all of which we have to remove.

Lines
It's hard to believe that someone would hit the carriage return or make some other kind of forced break at the end of every line, but it happens, because there are people who never had an opportunity to learn how to use computers properly. Remove these carriage returns, or ask someone who understands word processing to do the job for you.

Fonts
Fancy fonts may look lovely on your screen but we may not have that font, and most fonts are copyright protected. Use Times New Roman in twelve point, as it is easy for us to read on a screen and on paper, and perhaps something like Arial for sub headings. Try not to use more than two fonts in the book. If you do need some fancy styling, send us an example in a separate file. We may well have a similar font in stock, but buying a font set, sometimes costing £100 or more, for one project isn't worthwhile.

Photos and other artwork
All artwork will end up as CMYK or B&W TIFF files (don't get nervous - just submit either original photos / artwork or digital items in JPG format). Colour and greyscale images require 300 dpi resolution (dpi / ppi = dots / pixels per inch), while black and white graphics and line art must be at least 600 dpi. Don't *enlarge*

anything - the quality becomes unusable. Use only images that are at least the right size for your book.

If the above paragraph is incomprehensible, email us and tell us what artwork you have available.

Headings
Make chapter headings, sub-headings and subsidiary headings clear. It doesn't matter how you express them as long as you are consistent throughout the book.

Line spacing
You can use any line spacing you like, and if you email a book as an attachment, you will probably find it best to use single line spacing. It's easy for us change it at our end.

Dialogue
Take care when writing dialogue. Browse a decent book on your own bookshelf or in a bookshop and copy its style. You can use single or double inverted commas, but please be consistent throughout the book.

Timeline
You can't have someone falling pregnant at Christmas and having the baby at Easter. Take time to check dates and times of events. When writing about the past, check your facts.

Commas and house styles
When you were at school, your teachers probably told you never to use a comma before or after "and" or "but". Don't worry too much about this as long as your MS is easy to read.

Despite what your teacher told you or what is said in writing magazines, it is all right to start an occasional sentence with a conjunction, such as "and" or "but", although you shouldn't make a habit of it.

All right and alright
"Alright" is only all right when used in dialogue, otherwise always use "all right".

Spell and grammar check
Use the spell and grammar check feature in your word processor as you go along and give the whole book another thorough going over with the spell and grammar check when it is finished. This is essential.

More help
- Visit www.theeditorsblog.net or one of the many other advice sites for more advice and information.
- Borrow books on grammar from your library or look for sources online.

Publisher's jargon
- MS is short for manuscript.
- A font is a typeface. An alphabetical set of characters, all of one design style.
- Justification is where the lines of text are vertically even on the right side rather than ragged. Another way of expressing it is that the text is vertically aligned on both the left and right sides of the page. It is used in books, but please don't use it in your MS. Justification will be added during the page layout
- Line spacing is the space between consecutive lines.

Editing and Preparation

EDITING OVERVIEW

The word "editing" covers a multitude of activities - some minimal and others extensive, some necessary, others optional. Traditional publishers edit every book that they publish, and professional authors are aware that their work will be edited. The details itemised below describe the different kinds of editing that exist.

EDITING DETAILS

Assessment for suitability
At Stellium, we always glance though a MS to ensure that it isn't libellous, racist, obscene and so on, and to see what the author is trying to achieve. This is free of charge.

Formal assessment or critique
We don't offer this service, but you can find adverts for it in writing magazines and on the Internet. We believe that too much criticism can be disheartening, and obviously the critic will charge for the service.

Spell check
We will run a computer spell check for free. If any more work needs to be done, there will be a charge, but rest assured, we don't run up any costs unless we have your prior approval. See all our charge rates in the separate Price Guide.

Copy editing

This is optional. A copy editor checks for typing errors and errors in spelling, punctuation and grammar. She also checks chapter headings, headings within the book and so on. The editor may point out passages that don't make sense or that are obviously wrong. We charge from around £10 per 1,000 words, but you can avoid this expense by doing all of the following:

- Run a computer spell and grammar check on the whole manuscript.
- Print your MS out on paper in one-and-a-half spacing, as you will see more errors that way than you see on a screen.
- Ask a couple of friends to go over your MS for you and mark their corrections in red ink, then do the corrections yourself on your computer.
- Then, do another spell and grammar check.

Structural editing

This is optional. Structural editing is a highly skilled job that can amount to rewriting a book. If the book is non-fiction, the editor may send you a long list of queries about the things you say in the book, but if it is fiction, she will suggest reorganising chapters, cutting unnecessary detail, ensuring that names are consistent, that dates match up and much, much more. This will cost at least £10 per 1,000 words, so the more you can do yourself the better. Here are a few suggestions that help you avoid this expense:

- Take a trip to your local library and borrow books on fiction or non-fiction writing, as required. Read them and check what the writers say while simultaneously correcting your own MS on screen.
- Put the manuscript aside for a few days to allow you to step back from it, then print it out and check it on paper.
- Ask a couple of friends to go over the book for you.

Preparation

After editing, we email the file back to you while it is still in MS Word. You can make small changes at this point, but if you make major alterations, the whole project may have to be redone at your expense.

We now design the layout, set up the page formatting, typeset the text and finalise whatever else has been requested. We then send you a printout of the final page proofs for a final check. Changes by this stage should only be minor and any major changes will be charged out at £30 per hour. Major changes to a non-fiction book can put illustrations, tables, diagrams and so forth so far out of position that the whole job might need to be done again. Remember, you are the publisher and it is you who will bear the cost of redoing the typesetting.

This is where the publishing process becomes more professional, because MS Word or other word processing programs shouldn't be used for formal book publishing. Yes, many of these programs can save your manuscript as a PDF file, but there are still hidden gremlins that can upset the printer's digitisation process. Professional publishing houses use special page layout software for the design and typesetting stage of the work.

Beware of the over-enthusiastic friend

Some authors get so excited when they see their MS beginning to look like a real book that they show the page proofs to a friend. One friend or another may decide that he or she is a better judge of the content than the author, and pressurise the author to make major changes. If this happens to you, ask yourself whether your friend really is trying to help, or just enjoying the creative process himself without having to bother with the strain of writing his own book. Everybody has their own viewpoint, and this may work for that person, but not necessarily for you.

Even when the friend is truly well-meaning, things can go badly wrong. We remember a writer whose American friend took it upon herself to rewrite much of the author's book, so it ended up with some parts in US spelling and style while others were in UK spelling and style!

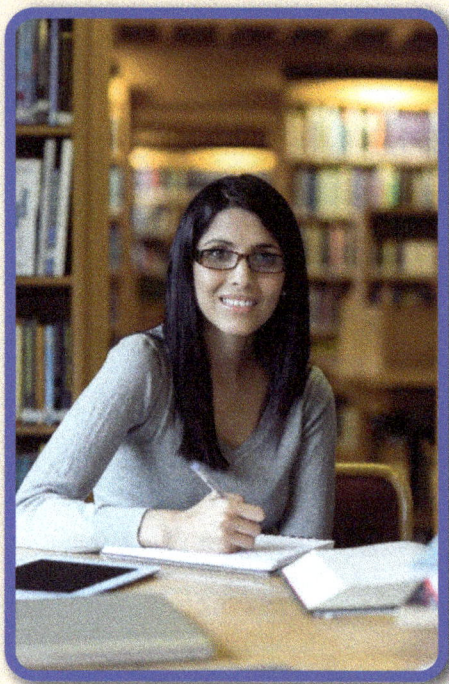

The Title and Covers

You will need to choose a title for your book, and a suitable cover. There are as many ways of going about this as there are authors, while different genres require different cover designs. Some authors have definite ideas about covers while others don't. If you aren't sure, ask us for suggestions. We can design something for you or we can work with your design and accommodate your ideas as far as practicable.

DETAILS

The cover

The cover will be in full-colour. It should catch the eye and it should suit the genre of the book. If you have some idea of what you want, let us know and if it's feasible, we will create the cover and send you a preview for review. You can have a hard cover, or a paperback, and the surface can be in gloss or matte laminate.

The book cover is an important part of the overall design, as it is the first part of the book that a potential reader sees. The construction of a good cover involves matching its looks to the genre of the subject matter, current trends in design and artwork, and choice of fonts as well as the choice of a title. The title should reflect the subject, whether fiction or non-fiction, and preferably contain key words relating to the subject of the book.

We often find that authors, magazine designers and artists are terrific in their own fields but they don't necessarily come up with successful book covers. One common problem is to try and put too much into a cover and make it look too "busy".

The title

Choose a title and a couple of backup title ideas, then check www.amazon.co.uk and www.amazon.com to see whether your favourite title is already being used or not. There is no copyright on titles, so in theory you could call your book "War and Peace", but by choosing something already in existence, your promotion and sales efforts may boost someone else's book rather than yours. Keywords are used by Google and other search engines to push the book forward when a person is looking for a specific kind of book online. Aside from the actual title (and subtitle if used), seven keywords can be added to a book's metadata in an ebook, but the title is the best place to insert one or more keywords.

Not quite sure about that? Well, here's a typical example. Type in the "cleverly" worded title: *A Stitch in Time Saves Nine* in the book searchbox on Amazon and press enter. Assume that your book is a crime thriller and the story's main thrust is about speedy ways of catching a murderer. We did this today and the following results immediately popped up:

A book entitled: *A Stitch in Time Saves Nine: the chances for successful preventive diplomacy in Zimbabwe.*

In second place and the rest of the list was a range of children's books on various subjects.

A Google search for the above title phrase brings up many references to dictionary and other definitions of the phrase, and adverts for sewing kits, needles and scissors.

Another disadvantage of a "clever" title ("clever" used to be a good idea years ago) is that no one is likely to look for that specific wording when searching for a thriller, anyway. Some keywords that our example could have had are: crime, thriller, murder, speedy arrest, and so on. A well-established and very popular author can get away with an obscure or even meaningless title, as the book will sell off the author's name as a search term anyway.

Once your book has been published, the whole title will form a key search phrase for anyone who already knows the title of your book, so it's a good idea to let people know the precise title of your book, so they know what to look out for on the 'Net. Add it to your email signature, use it in your Twitter and Facebook accounts, and you could also promote the book in a website - set up a website for free on www.wordpress.com and add a cover image, a synopsis and quotes from the book. If creating a website is not one of your skills, then talk to us.

We can embed a number of keywords into a print book's metadata - let alone an ebook - using features in our page layout and typesetting software, whereas the average person creating a PDF file from a word processor may not be able to do this.

Keep your title fairly short if possible and use a sub-title if appropriate. On the other hand, some authors use long titles in order to bring up as many keywords as possible. This may work in an online search, but it may put people off in a bookshop, where a cumbersome title is immediately recognisable as a ploy.

Back cover blurb
Nobody spends much time reading blurb so keep yours short, sweet and relevant. If you have collected an endorsement or two from an expert or in a press review, you can include it on the cover.

Fonts for titles and author's name
The title should be large enough to stand out even at a distance, and while fancy fonts can look great on your screen, they may be hard to read, especially on the spine of the book. Very often, the font should suit the genre of the book. Look at romance or fantasy

titles which tend to use fancy / italicised fonts, or business books which often capitalise the whole title in a plain font.

Overall

In general, it's probably easiest to choose an appropriate title and leave the rest to us, including fonts, etc.

Publisher's jargon

Metadata: data / words that provide information about other data. Commonly used online for search purposes. "Meta" originates from a root meaning "transcending", thus reflecting its unseen yet super-important nature.

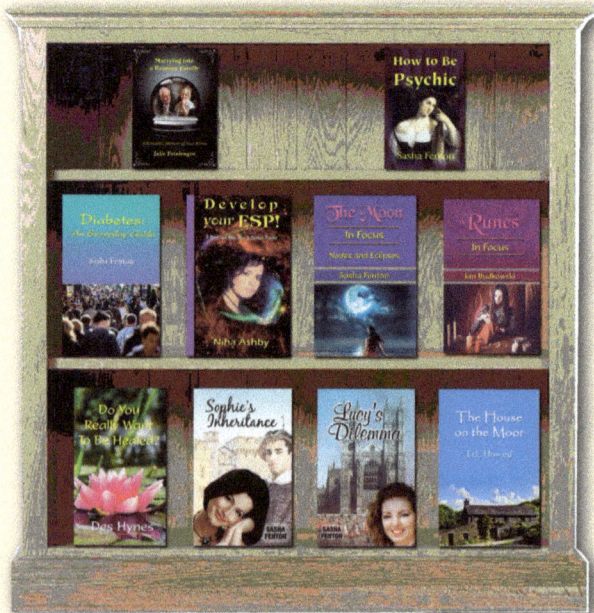

Printing

OVERVIEW

You are welcome ask us for anything, but there is a limit to what can be done by print-on-demand. The saying: "the impossible we do at once, miracles take a bit longer" applies nowadays, but there are some limits! We will be happy to tell you whether what you have in mind can or cannot be done. Here are some things that are available:

- Full colour content with either gloss or matte laminate cover.
- A hardback.
- A cloth covered (casebound) book.
- Various sizes and shapes of book. At present, not in landscape format.
- Variations in paper type and thickness.
- Digital colour printing inside your book.
- Printer's archive of your book for reprinting at any time. A small annual fee is involved.

DETAILS

Paper
Our printer uses very good, long-life, archive quality paper, and for a black and white book, you can choose white or cream paper. Cream paper is slightly thicker than the white paper, thus giving a small book more bulk, but white is the most popular colour.

For full-colour content, there are three qualities of paper to choose from. If your book is heavily coloured or illustrated, you will need the top quality, as this will best prevent the illustrations from showing through to the other side of the paper.

Recycled paper isn't used for most books - the quality is just not good enough, especially for archive quality requirements. Nowadays, most printers use carefully sourced paper.

Printing

When we know the size and scope of your book, we can tell you how much it will cost for the quantity of books you wish to print.

There is a one-off printer's setup fee to pay (currently £50 incl. VAT), and we always advise that you have an initial proof copy printed, so that you can check the cover and the insides of the "real" book. If you want to make changes, you can do so, but once the printer has set up your book, you will have to pay a second setup fee.

Once you are happy with the book, you can order as many or as few copies as you wish. Reprints usually take just a few days.

Sizes

Our printer can supply a number of book shapes and sizes, although landscape shapes are not available at present. Please ask us about size and shape, especially if you're planning full page illustrations for a children's book.

Archive

The printer will archive your book for as long as you need to keep it available. There is a small annual fee for this.

Overseas catalogue fee

If you're hoping to sell your book internationally, then you should consider a one-off advert in Ingram's worldwide catalogue.

Updating

If you produce technical manuals or books that need to be updated from time to time, the print-on-demand method is made for you, because you only print what you need when you need it, and you don't end up with hundreds of copies of out-of-date material lying around in your home. You can keep the same cover or change it, keep the same blurb or change it and you can certainly change the content.

There will be some costs, as the new material has to be partially or wholly re-typeset and designed, the printer's setup fee is charged again and you need a fresh proof copy to check over. Nevertheless, this is a great advance on the one-off method of printing, along with 6,000-copy or more print runs that used to be the norm.

Traditional litho printing is still available and has definite cost savings for large print runs, but the substantial financial outlay is only worthwhile if your book has already proved to be in great demand.

Something to add

If you want to add a CD or DVD to your book, you can buy plastic CD envelopes and stick the disc inside the back cover once your print order has arrived.

Costs

Prices change from time to time, so we use a separate, loose insert in this book. We can also discuss what is available and we can quote you separately for colour content or a non-standard size product.

Note that where printing is concerned, everything has to be paid for in advance, including our 15% admin fee, so put money aside for your print requirements.

Children's Books

A large number of people want to write children's books, and many can draw and paint lovely illustrations, but sadly, the chances of an agent or publisher taking them on are almost certainly zero. Publishers and agents receive many thousands of submissions each year and they rarely publish any of them - assuming they even have time to look at them - preferring instead to use tried and tested writers and illustrators, who know exactly what the publisher wants and can get it done in good time. For children's books, the only route is self-publishing. Nevertheless, there is always the chance of a brilliant book being picked up once it proves itself.

DETAILS

Most children's book writers don't want to produce large tomes, and to someone with no knowledge of publishing or even of printing, it looks as though a small colour-illustrated children's book should be cheap to produce due to its small size. In practice, a colour illustrated book involves a lot of precision work at the design and formatting stage, and timewise, this is costly. Once you get to the printing stage, the small size makes it economical to produce, while an ebook, of course, keeps going for nothing once it has been set up and published. Another great feature of ebooks is that the content can be in full colour for no extra cost, as no paper or real ink are involved.

Editing
If the book is a children's story in a similar format to a novel, all the

usual choices about editing apply. See the chapter on editing and preparation. If yours is an illustrated book with only a few words, please ensure that your spelling, grammar are good and that your story hangs together, as that way, there will be no need for editing.

Layout

This is a precision step, and you may need to send us sample drawings or page mock-ups of some kind so that we can produce what you want as accurately as possible.

Make a mockup

A mockup will give our techies an idea of what you have in mind, and we will produce a result as close as possible to your wishes.

Number the pages correctly, and show what is to go on the cover.

List the illustrations on a separate sheet and give them reference numbers connected to page numbers. Try labelling the images by using the image name plus a chapter number and consecutive number. For example, unicorn 1-1, deer 1-2, house 2-1, garden 2-2.

Then, insert a marker such as, "zzz unicorn 1-1" in the MS text, exactly where the image needs to be, Alternatively, stick post-it notes on the backs of your paper illustrations and other material to tell us precisely where they have to go.

It might be worth photocopying a few pages from a similar book to yours, and sending that to us as an example to show us clearly what you have in mind. Remember that it's difficult to convey pictures and layout from one person's mind to someone else's.

Techie matters

You will need to talk to our techie department about scanning, resolution, colour and so on, as there are a number of issues to take into consideration with regard to illustrations.

Ideally, send us original drawings / images and let us scan them in. That way, we can also enhance them at the same time if necessary, and we know exactly what colour-space, file format and resolution will work best for each individual image. Insure any valuable items, and if possible, keep backup copies of everything you send us. We will return all items to you once we have digitised them.

The book will be a multiple of four pages, e.g. 16, 22, 24 and so on, but that will include the copyright page, title page and possibly one or two other things as well. Our techies will help you with such matters.

Size, shape and more
Our children's books can be portrait in shape with a minimum trim size of 5" x 8" or square with a minimum size of 8" x 8", with either a hard cover or a paperback one. Talk to us before plunging ahead with drawings, paintings and graphics. The items have to be of a suitable size and shape for the purpose, so a landscape painting half the size of the intended book cover / page is not going to work out very well.

Marketing and sales
The same parameters apply to children's books as to any other type of book. See the chapter on promoting and marketing.

VERY IMPORTANT!

- Photocopy everything, always backup everything.
- Only send original work if we ask for it, but that does enable us to get the best out of your artwork.
- Don't post originals out to anybody in the run-up to Christmas.
- At other peak mail times, use a courier and perhaps also insure the material.

Admin and Legal

OVERVIEW

There are a few legal matters that have to be dealt with, and others that may not be necessary.

DETAILS

Legal deposits
It's mandatory to furnish the British Library (and possibly five other deposit libraries) with any book published for public consumption. We deal with this requirement for you.

Copyright
We will put a copyright page into your book showing the writer, illustrator and any other relevant contributor(s). Please ensure that everything in your book is yours or that you have written permission (a release form) from authors and/or publishers for written or illustrated work that isn't your own creation, from musicians and publishers for words to songs and for anything you have taken from the Internet. We will need the release forms for our files before we can proceed with your project.

Reversion of rights
If your book has been previously published or self-published elsewhere, we can advise you about reversion of rights. Other than in exceptional circumstances, you should already own the copyright to the text and possibly also any illustrations, but you will

have licenced it to the previous publisher, so the format of the finished book may not belong to you. You need to clear this before you can republish. Read your original contract thoroughly, and send us a photocopy for reference. It isn't difficult to get your rights back, and we can show you how to go about this.

ISBN (International Standard Book Number)

- If you want your book to be available to actual bookshops, online stores and individual people all over the world, you will need an ISBN. There are considerations as to whether you buy one ISBN, a set of them, or have your book published under our name. For an ISBN in our name, the project must be of a high enough standard to be acceptable to high street bookshops. Amazon is a different matter entirely, so don't fret about ISBNs for Kindle ebooks. Discuss the pros and cons with us and we will organise an Amazon ASIN number for your ebook.
- We will arrange a bar code for you for no extra charge, if an ISBN is involved.

Promoting and Marketing

OVERVIEW

Large conventional publishers invest money and effort in only a handful of books each year - usually when a film or television tie-in is already in the bag - therefore, most conventionally published books only make modest sales while many others sell next to nothing. It isn't well-known, but less than half of all publishers' books make a profit – in many cases, only after the second print run. This chapter covers a range of suggestions, some of which are easy to achieve and others that will need a fair bit of effort.

In both our conventional Mind, Body and Spirit (MB&S) publishing company, Zambezi Publishing Ltd, and our non-MB&S, ebook and self-publishing company, Stellium Ltd, the authors who have sold best are those with regular radio programmes on the BBC or those who went out and about month in and month out, giving talks about their specialist subjects along with those who sold books to their clients. A recent magazine interview with a million copy-selling author showed that she had retired from her normal job, allowing her to spend up to fourteen hours a day for months on end, promoting and marketing her books! Regular blog, Facebook, and Twitter posts, along with many other direct sales efforts did the trick for this author, but it shows just how hard the competition is nowadays.

An ISBN

If you want your paper book to be available to bookshops anywhere in the world, it will need an ISBN, (International Standard Book Number) and we can arrange this for you. If your book is only for friends and family or direct sales to your customers, you won't want this extra expense.

Kindle ebooks
An ebook is instantly available everywhere and it doesn't need an ISBN. Talk to us.

Approach
Whether you want to sell to the world in general or to a small number of people who will benefit from the specific information in your book, the same things apply:

- Make sure all your publicity information gives the ISBN, price and information about where to obtain your book.
- Define the readership for your book and work out where those people are likely to gather. You will gain a better idea of where and how to promote and sell your book.
- Consider your book's unique selling points and make the most of them wherever you can.
- Give talks at seminars in the same field as yours and put on Power-point presentations that are really interesting.
- Give everyone present at any suitable event a leaflet or postcard showing your book's cover and giving the ISBN, price and places where the book can be purchased.
- Be pleasant... even to those who irritate you.

DETAILS AND SUGGESTIONS

Press release - leaflets and information
We can produce a press release for you. We charge a small fee for the work, but once you have it, you can alter it to suit any occasion and you can make as many copies as you want. You can give copies to the media, your local bookshop or library, your club or society and your friends.

If you decide to make up your own press release, make up some kind of eye-catching headline with a few words about the book, a little bit about yourself and an endorsement or two if you have them.

We can create postcards with your book cover on one side and blurb and relevant details on the other side. The same goes for bookmarks with a thumbnail of your book cover, a little blurb and the relevant sales details.

Libraries

Some libraries are happy to take a couple of copies of your book for their shelves, while others are not. They won't pay for the books, but at least it helps to get your work out there, and it might encourage others to buy your book. You may be able to persuade your library to allow you to give a talk - but once again, this depends on the local library manager, as some are cooperative and others are not.

If you need a few extra books printed for such an event, please order them from us in good time.

Ask your library which wholesaler supplies them with their stock and contact us to see if we can get your books into that wholesaler, as they might also supply further libraries around your area in particular, and the country in general.

Local shops

Some local shops will be happy to stock your book, and some will put on author events. On the other hand, some aren't interested, but you should ask or you'll never find out. If you need extra copies of your books for an event, please order them from us in good time. We can supply leaflets, postcards and bookmarks for you. Even W. H. Smith may buy the odd book directly from an author as long as it relates to local history or local matters in some way.

Bookshop databases

We can purchase bookshop address lists for you and send information to every shop in the country, or to bookshops that specialise in your book's genre.

Coping with book signings

The popular image of an author sitting at a table behind piles of his book, and a queue of eager fans waiting to speak to the author and get signed copies is only likely to happen if the author is a celebrity. If you do anything in a shop or library, it's best to have some kind of talk or demonstration prepared well in advance, and make sure that the bookshop advertises your event for a couple of weeks beforehand; a note in the window just a day or two before your talk isn't going to be much use.

Make up a poster advertising your book and plenty of leaflets or postcards promoting your book, and give them to the shop at least a couple of weeks before the event.

Book launch

- If you want to throw a party to launch your book, please do so. You may be able to arrange this at a local library or bookshop, or perhaps even a local tourist venue. You can invite the local press and representatives and other useful people to your party. Send out flyers at least four weeks in advance and send press releases to the local media. Make sure that you have plenty of books on hand to sell, by ordering them a month in advance of the date of the event. Prepare drinks, not forgetting soft drinks and water, and buy in some tasty tit-bits for people to nibble.
- Prepare talks, Power-point presentations, readings and demonstrations in advance and rehearse them thoroughly before the event.
- If you can introduce some kind of audience-participation into your talk, so much the better.
- Ensure that everyone signs the visitor's book, giving their name, address and email.

- After the event, send thank you notes to everyone who attended. Show the book details on that note as well.
- Don't forget to thank and reward the bookshop or library staff or anyone else who has helped you. Maybe give them a box of chocolates as a mark of gratitude.
- If it is likely that the shop or tourist shop will buy copies of your book to sell on to their own customers, offer them a trade discount, typically up to 40%. Ask what trade discount they normally get, and even if it is as high as 50%, give it to them. Just make sure that you cover your book printing expenses, as there's no point in selling at a loss unless it's a temporary book promotion using a limited amount of stock.

Book festivals
- Local book festivals would be great promotional events in which to participate, but contact the organisers months in advance, as they plan their programme long before the date. Some are more co-operative than others, but you won't know unless you ask.
- Send in a proposal of what you will speak about. If you are prepared to take a stand, maybe share the cost and the effort of doing the event with one or two other authors.
- See whether your local book festival gives opportunities to local authors and find out how to apply.
- Smile at people but don't pounce on them. Offer sweets, postcards, bookmarks or anything else that will encourage interest in your work.
- Have a notice board on your stand showing times and details of mini-events, such as when you will be reading from your book, and give demonstrations, advice or anything else that will make your stand interesting.

Amazon
Once your book is published, we will make it and/or your ebook available around most of the world via Amazon and also available to other online bookshops as well as normal high street bookshops.

Magazines

Send local magazines and newspapers a leaflet about your book, and follow up anything you send with a phone call. Put some effort into checking the magazine's website, which will usually tell you where or to whom to send your information. If you address things to a person by name, they will be more inclined to read your leaflet.

You might be able to write an article on your subject for a magazine, while also advertising your book in the magazine. Some magazines will want you to buy a month's worth of advertising in exchange for accepting the article, and you may consider this a useful thing to do. Others will want you to give several copies of your book away to their readers. If you do this, keep the names and addresses of those who write in asking for free copies, as you may be able to post further information out to them later, but do bear in mind that those who routinely send off for "freebees" aren't likely to spend actual money on buying books. If you phone a magazine to follow something up, be friendly but keep things short and sweet, and make sure you phone the right person – by name, if at all possible. Ensure the magazine has your contact details.

Websites

There are websites devoted to showing and selling books. Addresses change frequently, so we don't list such websites in this book.

If you don't have a website of your own, it's worth talking to us, as we can design, set up and maintain a simple website for you. The costs are affordable, both the set up and a regular monthly or quarterly maintenance fee.

Emails

Add a colourful signature to your email address and a line about your book(s). Avoid logos or book covers though, as this counts as spam.

Amazon and Google promotions

Both www.amazon.co.uk and all its sister sites around the world sell paper books as well as Kindle ebooks. They offer a "look inside" facility that allows readers to view a few pages of your book. If you have a Kindle ebook as well as a paper version, the "Look Inside" feature will install automatically. Without an ebook, we can still arrange this for you.

Amazon or Google adverts or promotion aren't free, there are variable "click-through" costs, and there is no guarantee that the person looking at the advert will buy the book. We haven't found these to be very helpful, because there are so many people using the systems, and many of them are also willing to pay high prices for clicks. This kind of promotion is perhaps better used only if your book is already showing decent sales.

AMS

Amazon Marketing Services is a recent innovation that works for books signed up to KDP select, which we can arrange for you. The AMS service will run a campaign directed at people who buy books similar to yours, for a fee. At present, this service only addresses the USA market, and not the UK. Nevertheless, sales are sales, wherever they take place.

Fiverr.com

www.fiverr.com is an amazing website which you can use to promote your book, but it is also great if you are looking for someone to design a book cover, illustrate, create cartoons, edit and more for reasonable prices.

Facebook, Twitter, Pinterest, Instagram

You can show the cover of your book and write about it on all these sites, and it is a useful way of keeping your book in front of the world. Make sure to include a link or path to where your book can be purchased - Amazon or your own website, for example.

Reviews
Ask everyone you know to buy a copy of your paper or ebook from www.amazon.co.uk and to leave a review. If they don't want to write an actual review, they should at least give it a star rating.

Notification
We will notify Amazon and its various branches worldwide, www.abebooks.com, Ingrams (wholesaler), Nielsen Book Data and other retail databases in the USA about your book.

Goodreads, Wordpress and so on
You can write a blog on www.wordpress.com and you can advertise your book on Goodreads. New authors often give away books through Goodreads, and while this is often mooted as a good idea, our experience is that it is an expensive waste of time. The recipients are likely to be in the USA, so the cost of postage needs to be added to the cost of the book, and we found that after sending out a dozen or so copies of a book, we did receive a few very nice reviews, but no sales resulted from this at all.

Blogs
You can set up a blogging website and collect the names of people who read your blog. Create and send out email newsletters.

Mail Lists
Campaign Monitor or Mail Chimp will help you create and use mail lists. If you bring out more than one book, contact everyone who has reviewed your previous book and offer them a freebee paper book or ebook if they will do another review.

Radio stations
Both the BBC and independent radio stations used to offer authors

opportunities to talk about their books, but this rarely happens now. If you do get asked to broadcast, the following ideas will help:

- Send a copy of the book to the radio station in good time so the presenter can at least read the blurb and the author page.
- Practise recording at home before the event and learn how to improve your performance.
- Radio stations are often hard to find, so go there a few days before the event, to make sure you know where it is and where to park.
- Be early.
- Dress nicely but don't overdo it.
- Ask them to give you a CD of the programme to listen to later, or get a friend to record the programme. This way, you will be able to correct mistakes and do better the next time.
- Send a thank you card to the operations people and the presenter after the event.

Lending rights
PLR is short for Public Lending Right. Any author can sign up to this and receive payment for the books borrowed from public libraries. Visit www.plr.uk.com

ALCS, the Authors' Licensing and Collecting Society, which passes money directly to the authors from photocopies that are made in libraries and colleges in the UK and throughout Europe. Visit www.alcs.uk.com

A local event
Get to know other local authors and put on an author's event at a local gallery, coffee shop, a room over a pub, a sports club, your church or some other symbiotic venue. Ask them to bring their friends and relatives, as this will introduce them to your book, while you get to see theirs and talk to them about their experiences. Spread the word in any way that you can.

And finally...

Always keep a couple of copies of your book handy - for example, in the boot of your car - along with flyers and post cards if you have them. Do this even when you go on holiday, as you never know who might take an interest in what you do. Shops in foreign holiday locations are unlikely to be helpful, as they specialise in maps, local interest booklets and second hand books, and they can be indifferent to the point of rudeness to writers and publishers who pop in to speak to them.

Having said this, most marketing gets you out there to meet people and to see something of the world away from your computer, and that can't be bad.

Contact Us

Here are our contact details. We prefer email to phone calls, because we then have time to research your enquiry if it's a complex one. Nevertheless, you may have questions that need a phone call, so don't hesitate to call us.

Stellium Ltd
22 Second Avenue,
Camels Head,
Plymouth
Devon PL2 2EQ
Tel: 01752 367 300
Fax: 01752 350 453
Email: stelliumpub@gmail.com

Registered in England no: 08348708

Speak to, or email:
Sasha Fenton
Email: sashafenton01@gmail.com

Or:
Jan Budkowski
Email: janbud@gmail.com

Addendum: Sample "Think Form"

We always ask for a Think Form before we quote on a project, so a current version is shown below. It shows you most of what we need to know, but very importantly, it helps you to think about what you really want from your project!

Don't pull out these pages - fill out the information called for on a separate page (mentioning each question as well as your answer) in the order below, and send it to us, preferably by email. You may find an A4 Think Form insert in this book and if so, just fill that in and send it to us at the address on the previous page. Keep a copy for yourself. Alternatively, ask us to send you a printed copy.

THIS IS OUR (SAMPLE) "THINK-FORM"

This form does not commit you to anything - it enables us to gain some knowledge of your intentions and it gives you an opportunity to think things through.

BLOCK LETTERS PLEASE

Full Name: ....

Residential Address: ....

....

....

Email: .... Telephone: ....

Sample "Think Form"

PLEASE TELL US ABOUT YOUR MANUSCRIPT OR PROJECT

(If you're not sure about any question, please say so, and leave it blank)

Your book's working title: _____

(You may want to change this later; this isn't irrevocable.)

NOTE: Please check Amazon.co.uk and Amazon.com to ensure that your title doesn't already exist. Also, try to keep your title short and related to the book's subject matter, Try to include keywords.

Subtitle if needed: _____

Author/s full names: _____

Do you need a "professional" quality book, or just something to give your friends and family, as a family memoir, or to use in conjunction with your business? _____

Think hard about your real needs and what you really want to spend.

Genre: _____

(e.g. fiction, training manual, memoir, poetry, etc.)

If non-fiction, what is the subject? _____

Approx. No. of graphics: _____

Approx. No. of photos: _____

Approximate number of words. You'll find this by using your word-count facility: _____

Are you submitting a cover design or do you want us to make one up for you? _____

A rough idea of the size of book, e.g. 5" x 8", etc. _____

((We can suggest an appropriate size.)

Do you need colour inside your book? Bear in mind this significantly increases printing costs: _____

Does your work only need a quick once over, a more detailed edit, or professional quality structural editing? _____

Do you want an ebook in addition to a print book, and do you want it straight away or later? _____

Do you only want an ebook? _____

Do you want a hard cover or a paperback? _____

Do you fancy a shiny or a matte-laminate finish? _____

(Both the shiny and matte cost the same.)

Note that we also recommend a photo of the author/s, some bio about the author/s and some "blurb" about the book for the back cover.

We can help with the "blurb".

Do you need an ISBN? _____

Do ask us about anything, as we're here to help.

Sample "Think Form"

Our contact details:

Stellium Ltd
22 Second Avenue,
Camels Head,
Plymouth
Devon PL2 2EQ
Tel: +44 (0)1752 367 300
Fax: +44 (0)1752 350 453
Email: stelliumpub@gmail.com

Registered in England no: 08348708

Most publishing projects nowadays don't require a meeting.
If you feel that your project is exceptional,
kindly email us, with details, to arrange an appointment.

Here's a final tip:
We are more than happy to speak to anyone on the phone,
but an email is more useful - spoken details are soon forgotten,
whereas an email can be referred to, even months later.
We have a rule, never to commit to anything verbally.

We hope that this book has helped you to understand the ins and outs of the publishing trade more fully, because, if you are really keen about writing, then you want to know your trade reasonably well. This is as important to an author as the parallel is to a chef, a solicitor, a brain surgeon or a chicken farmer.

At Stellium, we try to help our self-pub authors, and our traditional ones, and we love to see happy smiles when a book has finally completed the publishing process and has landed in the author's lap, so to speak!

You are welcome to ask us about the best course of action for your project, and we'll happily advise you according to our experience and the current state of the book trade.

Don't forget that we also have a sister company that complements Stellium Ltd - Zambezi Publishing Ltd, which publishes Mind, Body and Spirit titles conventionally (i.e. not self-publishing), so if you have an idea for a fairly New Age kind of How-To book that has a different take on the subject, then tell us about it - you never know, it may be just what we need at that moment. Email us a synopsis and two chapters for our perusal.

Index

Index

Index

www.ingramcontent.com/pod-product-compliance
Lightning Source LLC
Chambersburg PA
CBHW040122070426
42448CB00042B/3342